POWERS *and* BOUNDARIES

POWERS *and* BOUNDARIES

Poems

THOMAS REITER

LOUISIANA STATE UNIVERSITY PRESS *Baton Rouge* 2004

Manufactured in the United States of America
First printing

Designer: Melanie O'Quinn Samaha
Typeface: Minion
Printer and binder: Thomson Shore, Inc.

Library of Congress Cataloging-in-Publication Data:

Reiter, Thomas.
Powers and boundaries : poems / Thomas Reiter.
p. cm.
ISBN 0-8071-2999-2 (alk. paper) — ISBN 0-8071-3000-1 (pbk. : alk. paper)
I. Title.
PS3568.E526P69 2004
811'.54—dc22

2004005136

The paper in this book meets the guidelines for permanence and durability of the Committee on Production Guidelines for Book Longevity of the Council on Library Resources. ♾

The author offers grateful acknowledgment to the following publications, in which some of the poems herein originally appeared, sometimes in a different form: *Appalachia, Asphodel, Caribbean Writer, Chariton Review, Crab Orchard Review, Crazyhorse, Folio, Georgia Review, Gettysburg Review, Great River Review, Kunapipi, Laurel Review, Literary Review, New Madrid, Pinyon, Poetry Daily, Poetry Northwest, Revista/Review Interamericana, Southern Review, Tar River Poetry,* and *Texas Review.*

The author also wishes to thank the McMurray-Bennett Foundation for its generous support during the writing of this book.

For Jo Nell,
Peter and Jill,
and Alicia and Rowan

Contents

POWERS *and* BOUNDARIES

At First Light in a Field

Webs of the orb-weavers
rolled out of summer this far
and no farther. Radii
glow like particle tracks

in a proton collider, meaning
a grand unification theory
may be on its way. On thorn
bushes are egg masses
like flower pots, like feathers,

like tiny hedgehog brooches—
a five & dime, but not
open this hour. Moisture
building out of the earth

from a root crystal makes frost
clouds that displace their weight
in light, being the color
of French bread torn open
at the table and passed around.

On a granite boulder, moss
hunches up like a knapsack.
In it there's a map
to find this field again.

Buffalo Creek Flood, Logan County, West Virginia, 1972

No word came down to the children
playing on tree swings in the park,
kicking higher and higher and
catching snowflakes in their mouths,
nothing to prepare the way for
the rest of their lives, no word
at all from the mining company
that the creek water used to wash coal
uphollow, now a lake as deep as debt,
was pressing to collapse its slag
impoundment. What did come down
was taller than anyone's father
and more strict, a wave of mine waste
carrying the contents of a village
many had never visited. Mobile
homes and pickup trucks and cows
and a section of track that no one
would lay a penny on again,
and now children with their swings
and the oaks they were secured to—all
tumbling in the black roller through falling
snow and into the next company
town, where a few had friends or kin,
though no word came down to them.
Nothing like that day in anyone's
memory, and the miners' children
were there. . . . To those unharmed
in the hills the slag wave sounded
like a homecoming victory.

Washday, West Indies

She plunges whites and colors
into a clear pool the rainforest
river makes on its way to salt,
then kneads the clothes like bread dough—
this young woman who bends to
her place in the ordinary,
watching foam billow like cumulus
to the surface. She's
part of the river in the eye
of that frigate bird overhead,
wings like a pterodactyl's,
and a cry that makes a gull
release the inchling it skimmed
from the river, whereupon
the marauder snaps up that morsel
midair, then lands on the rooftree
of the house this woman's husband
raised: planking from storm-
wracked schooners, tidewrack
scavengings. Late at night after
love-making she can hear the sea
in that wood, but now she's climbing
the current, basket on hip,
placing colors and whites on boulders
to dry in the sun,
workday and Sabbath clothes needing
before dark to be shaken free
of the shapes of lava rock
and picked clean of the mountain's
waterborne seeds.

Spring Plowing: Great-Grandfather and the Second Wisconsin Cavalry

His knee let go a report like the plowshare
snapping a tree root, and now he comes to—
face down and choking on newly-turned earth,
on tendrils and grubs. He sits up and comes gasping
back to where the horse waits in her traces,
and so he dodges the weekly's obit:
"Joseph Mueller, Gardener, Answers Summons."

When he forces himself to unclasp his hands
from that knee, it's a sunburst of bones
with the Minié ball he took at Vicksburg
fifty years ago still nesting there. The relic
falls into his palm and he pockets it.
He binds the wound with his shirt then lies down,
faint in the cold furrow. Is that knob pressing
against the back of his neck last year's potato?
A bone thrust up by frost? Grant's campaign
in Mississippi is upon him again.

He remembers marveling how orchids rooted
in punkwood of old stumps that at home
grow lichen and puffballs. Chickasaw Bayou:
the corduroy road of tree trunks broke apart,
so this vegetable farmer from the headwaters
and horseman in the Second Wisconsin
led his mount through a new river world.

Suck-hole marshes with their will-o'-the-wisps
and alligators longer than the grave.
Spanish moss slathering across his face, cold
as corpse flesh, cold as the picket in a live
oak he homed in on by muzzle flash,
the sharpshooter in farmer's denim
who the next morning came crashing down on him
in a squall as he passed under that tree,
living and dead tangled in the black Chickasaw.

He unhitches the plow horse and climbs on.
Dusk, and the square-tipped rays of the common
blue chicory along the edge of the garden
are closing as he passes. He knows now
he'll watch this plot turn to bindweed.
And turn to the story of this wound
his daughter looking after him will hear, a way
he'll have then of looking after himself
to someone someday who will write it down.

Dusk too when he climbed onto a cypress knee
and tallied piles, diarrhea, palsy, memory loss
toward an early mustering out; the hour
reb jimsonweed blossomed, a foul sweetness
drawing moths to flutter before his eyes
while snipers settled beads into notches.
Surgeons found two Minié balls but missed
the one that would topple him at last
into his own furrow and this telling,
history's cunning with windage and distance.

Inventory

I pulled on the gloves of the one who
had gone before me, canvas gloves
like a railroad engineer's, then followed
below ground to plumbing supplies
in row upon row like library stacks
the summer I turned fifteen and was told,
"You'll become a man who can say
he's done inventory."

I clocked in when the offices closed,
went down to carved and dated initials
along a center beam, my own
in place at the end: inventory takers
this work had taken . . . where?
On break I paced the loading dock
and looked for light to go out of the sky
and light years to appear. I turned

"Love Me Tender" into "copper nipples,
angle valves, never let me go . . . ,"
and the rest of Top Forty rock and roll
into the whole time's worth of fittings,
but always went back to where stone walls
let through what looked like black jam
and corner seams kept squeezing out
incredible cheese. Couldn't something
that fattened off the foundation
be raising its young in my next bin?

While the watchman made his rounds
and the sump pump cycled on, I counted
elbows, locknuts, tees, everything
for journeywork into a barrel
one kind and size at a time
—by midnight I'd catch myself
tallying their shadows too—then

put them back to complete the circle
no one had ever departed from,
the hours going I couldn't see where
if not into song.

Kill-Devil

(St. Kitts, 1751)

A man awakens from rain that lifts coffins
from the family churchyard and launches them
into the sea, four generations of planters
pitching and yawing. No matter the dream,
he is lying inside mosquito gauze at dawn
in the great house at the center of drought.
He has sent his wife and children off-island.

The conch shell called Triton's Trumpet
awakens the slaves, who turn their lives over
to light. *The pulse is the soul of the arm.*
Why do Indian sayings come to him now?
Then he remembers. . . . *Will my right arm fail?*
is a master's version of the proverb.
Runaways hide in mountain caves where Carib
revenants are said to protect them, and even
overseers with hounds will not go there.

Plantation gardens wilt, the fowl die.
How is a master to feed his inheritance?
Or treat their fevers? The herbs themselves
perish: gully root for pounding to grains,
stalks of jumbie pepper for decoction.
He listens. Ah, mule cries at the mill.
Stone rollers, pressing juice from cane
for the boiling vats, make mosquito netting
tremble. A furnace vent's a bell.
Every dawn sound has its one job to do,
which is to reach him. *Yes. Yes. Yes.*

But if slaves have distilled the forbidden
kill-devil from sugar skimmings
and taken it by night to the caves. . . .
I did not choose this life.
The master's gauze fills like a sail
as he lies alert for undertones

and finds them in order on the trade wind:
a night-soil cart rolling toward the sea
and cassava root being grated for his bread.
He crosses himself to begin the day.

Wherryman

He'd be a common water strider
except this oval inch
of the order *Hemiptera*, "true bug,"
takes one world into another.
I watch from an overhanging bank

as he tilts through the surface
tension again and again, turning
this pool into stump rings until
thorax and abdomen lie inside

a pearly envelope of air. Awkward
as a man wearing a barrel,
he labors against buoyancy to climb down
a bur reed through sunlit water
where minnows flare away,

sparks from a grinding wheel,
then at last to grip the root
and suck decay from the stream bed.
I think abundance, economy . . .

and now, no longer shining,
the wherryman has to let go.
Spinning like a seed pod,
he lifts toward this world in which
the air I breathe has far to go.

The Tomb Closing and Repair Crew

1.

Three men in Public Works gray arrive
on their circuit of graveyards.
Today an aboveground vault
eroded by sea winds and scarred by tunnels
of those other workers, who connect

one darkness with another, who
build from the ground to an open seam
where the roof overhangs. Men
in the name of perpetual care
crowbar the concrete walls into plumb
for steel shims, and refacing follows.

Idling now against an empty marble
chamber newly in place and still
nameless, they pass a flask around
as the trade wind comes up, clacking
the arm-length pods of flamboyant trees
against one another. The men laugh—
mother-in-law's tongue scolding them.

2.

At the gates a hearse has caught fire,
so they come running with shovels
and inter the engine block. Smoke
hurries the pallbearers as they roll out
teak and ivory. The tombworkers wink
at one another: this has to be

Ervin Wheatley III, five terms
as councilman matching his jail time
for green-lighting ganja through the harbor.
It's as though he's coming out from
another deal-closing in clouds of cigar smoke
and onto the shoulders of voters.

Freight your own Carrara marble
while everyone else gets pale concrete,
then rig a mourning party,
good East Caribbean dollar going
for flowers, hymns, bowed heads.
Afterwards, gratis, the crew helps
push the smoldering hearse away.

3.

When the school bus drops their children off,
the men are building the back wall
that will seal the late Wheatley away.
Even the youngest boy wants to help
mix the mortar, though quickly all
turns are over, and the afternoon.

There's only time for children
to put their heads in the mouth
of the Lion of Judah
sculptured on a Rastafarian tomb;
to poke a finger through a wall
and listen to the skeleton's teeth
and dare one another, *Take a deep*
breath. They run back to where fathers

have given the councilman his final
trowel swipe. Heaped with hibiscus
and spider lily—they're plastic to last—
he's the whole show.

Exposures

Opening a road through wilderness
for the WPA, 1937, my father
in his twentieth year has gotten up
from the sawyer's position, a held

genuflection. He's no stranger to
the daylong rhythm a crosscut calls for,
how you pull and never push
so the blade won't buckle, twanging.

But now for the moment he's worked it
back out of heartwood (where
thorn shaped, square, and cloven teeth
paused) and holds it upright.

His bare arms glowing with the dust
of rings that set out to reach him there
long before he was born,
this woodsman who will die soon

on Corregidor is a gag musician.
To his father's souvenir German helmet
from the Argonne he's affixed branches like horns,
and now with one foot in his lunch pail

and one hand on his heart while the other
flexes spring steel, bringing out
fundamentals and overtones,
he is doing an aria from *Siegfried.*

Basso profundo, he accompanies himself
for his brother who will die at Anzio,
who is adjusting the bellows and lens
and bending in tears to the view finder.

Root Cellars

Wind in the mountain grasses moves through
the Temple of Fashion, its inventory
a dressmaker's wire form surrounded by
cuttings of late snow, its ridgepole
like the spine of a pack mule hauling
mother lode. Given to ghost towns,
I've stopped at the marker for Creed, Idaho,

P.O. EST. 1871, DISCONT. 1900. Silver
and cholera and more silver . . . and
at this elevation, beans for Sunday dinner
had to be started on Friday. The street
I'm taking slowly, Main Chance, ends among
cable spools and cog wheels and tailings
at a slope of boarded-over tunnels,
glory holes gone to glory.

Miners adding root cellars to their cottages
had to dig by stealth because the company owned
the earth below a depth of three feet.
Thresholds? Stepping across foundations
made of blasting debris and the one dream,
I can look straight into the secret:

no one owns this place to any depth.
The ads back East brought women, though
never enough. Boom times: among splayed boards
growing cup fungus and puffballs, I find
a metal sign on a tall rod for planting
by the front door. Its raised lettering says,
LUCKY MINER'S HOUSE BUT NO WIFE.

Set well back from the mules and mud,
this wall resembling a flight of stairs
—limestone quarried in Ohio—is Tabor House

after the mineowner. The wainscotted
outhouse with walnut seats for family
and pine for servants? No better darkness

for maids to drop broken crystal into.
The next lot, briars now and windblown
tin stamped with fleurs-de-lis, was kept
cleared for the tent services of Rev. Dyer,
a circuit rider who could double his
collection plate with fees for scrambling
up the terrain and dowsing ore deposits.

Prayer and pickaxe, thirty years, until
the best veins, the blossom rocks, played out
and the Bitterroot, Wenatchee & Pacific
pulled up its spur and Creed lost
the only female faro dealer in all of Idaho.

Powers and Boundaries

(Jamaica, 1880)

A rutted lane stretches through woodland
to a public wellstead, divides around it,
and continues on. Women are drawing water
for callaloo soup and for laundry they hang
in the trade winds that came ashore
bearing the Spanish Crown and the last things:
death, judgment, heaven, and hell.

Two figures approach the well: an old man
on muleback followed by a boy on foot.
Eleven years old, he pushes an umbrella stand
mounted on a caster, steering with
a curved handle affixed to the rim. Jutting
from shadow there, a saw handle, T square,
claw hammer, and the knob of a brace and bit,
while the rider carries tools in saddlebags.

The man reins up. And while he's pointing
off into the forest and saying a rare
mahogany tree grows there, and that he remembers
—it was the year before Abolition—
watching craftsmen from England plane and mortise
that wood, building a sideboard for china
in the great house of the sugar estate where,
a young man, he was a kitchen slave,
ragling boys leaning against the wellstone call
this one's name and wave. He lifts his free hand
to them but continues looking into the trees.

Master carpenter and apprentice, they do not
pause for water, they go on past to where
the boy is learning to come into
the powers and boundaries of the common
tamarind, white cedar, and whistling pine.
He loves to set each grain and fragrance free.
Snug the studding in and toenail, so. . . .

In framing out a dwelling, he has already
begun to take in what the man knows:
the discipline and beauty of angles made true,
the keeping quality of seasoned wood.

That Hunger

Old loaf-maker, your panel truck
stopped on our block, its horn
the glide of three notes from a roadster,
its motor like the sound of cards
when my father shuffled, the cut
riffling into a deck again.
Our street unplowed, my mother sent me
to you for the first time, only
my galoshes and your tire chains
meeting. Your parka made a cavern
as you bent down to ask my name.
"Harpo" you called me finally, then
turned the silver handles at the back
to part HUMPKE's on one door
from BREAD on the other. Drumming
your thumb on the bus driver's
changemaker looped to your belt
inches from my ear, did you think
I would never speak? I wanted
to stay among waftings of Humpke's
Bread warm and without end, shapes like
roundhouses and coach cars, bread
as deep as I could see:
rye, Vienna, sourdough, wheat,
my breath vanishing into theirs
and all of it into the snowy trees.
Imagine throwing open the doors
and finding a boy in the fresh bread.
"See you again," you said,
placing the loaves in my care.

A Charm for Your Doorstep

Any distance and from anywhere,
on the backs of beetles,
through the tracts of birds,
this flowering ground-cherry came
to set itself up in hardpan
at your back door. It gave you
where nothing else would
a white throat at each leaf axil,
then green sepals lanterning a nub.

Now those bladders are butcher paper,
falling, and overnight
turn to grillwork like panes of frost.
When snow collects in the throat
of the spider's web,
take the ground-cherry's pod
in your right hand.
Rattling its yellow seed, its power
against ill will and forgetfulness,
cast it in the cut your right heel makes.

And swear by the ten bowed ribs
of *Physalis subglabrata*
that its berry like a setting moon
is the grain of truth in everything.

Secret Readings

The way he tells it, the coveted stone
is compensation for all the blank
specimens of frost-heave in fields
that for fifty years he's scrabbled over
alone. Last autumn, uprooting
a maple from the scrap of tallgrass prairie
enclosing his parents' graves,
he found the slab covered with carvings
and sank it flush at his front door.

Now the university has heard about it,
so he's anything but alone.
The most he'll let the scholars do,
crouching in conference at his door,
is read the side open to the weather
and explain its language of runes,
how letters known by such names
as *wealth, ox, courage,* and *thorn*
can tell us this:
Eight Goths and twenty-two Norsemen
on an exploring journey from Vinland.
We were out and fished one morning
and when we returned to this spot
discovered nine of our men
red with blood and dead.
Ave Virgo Maria! Save us from evil!

And the message cut into the buried side?
Is more of their journey there? And the date?
There's nothing he wants to know
beyond that *Ave.* He tells them nothing
of the time a young man helping his father
break this Dakota prairie, five yoke of oxen
against the burls of rootstalk, saw fire coming
on the long grassland wind.
A lane plowed around the house and barn

held, but rolling smoke black as loam
maddened his mother, who ran
out of the circle, his father after her.

He buried them in flowering
milkweed and spurge and meadow rue
somehow spared. What could he do but stay,
his life harrowed and clarified
to a dream of running but never
crossing the rim of prairie?
The oaks undermined by fire fell
as loud as ordnance while he
plowed the burnt sod for winter wheat
and squared off the graveyard.

So now it pleases him to have
wealth and *ox* and *courage* and *thorn*
as threshold. Soon enough
the professors can say a prayer
over his grasslander's bones
and the bones of his parents lost to fire
and the bones of the Old World hacked to marrow
(*Ave Virgo Maria! Save us from evil!*)
then get their answers from the other side.

Fresh Fish

The seine's bellyful of shadows
hauled at first light onto the beach
becomes reef dwellers pouring their facets
over one another. Soon the gossamer net,
hung to dry between a coconut palm
and the furled mast of a catboat
run up on the sand, the *Lady Bountiful,*
St. Kitts & Nevis, flutters like
a kitchen curtain in the trade wind—
a sign saying open for business.
Women who come to this fisherman know
what he gives for good measure.
Reaching back over the gunnel, he picks
one of each kind he's caught, runs
a stick like a teacher's pointer
through their gills, and resting one end
on his shoulder while holding the other
at arm's length, displays his fresh
array. He tells of linen-skinned mullets
to be curried; moonbass for grilling
with plantains or deepening the stock pot;
and sunset groupers, an orange path
head to tail on carbon-dark scales:
poach them in water brought to trembling.
Moving now in a depth of his own
making, he tells of the barrier reef
that calms the waters these live in.
Ordinary coral antlers and pillows,
yes, but today while spreading his net
he saw candelabras with polyp mouths
in place of flames . . . colonies
of deadmen's fingers clutching at treasure . . .
vermilion sponges shaped into bowls
and vases . . . tall chimneys where
the stars abide. . . . The story ends
and women step from the sea to supper.

Furrows

What luck in a wheat field
for the boy hearing his name called.
What other moments can he point to?
That no one caught him jamming an apple
into the tailpipe of the scoutmaster's coupe
or touching the communion wafer
stuck to the roof of his mouth?

Snow is falling in the Great Depression
on fathers and sons forming a circle
as they do this April day each year,
inside it a dozen foxes and now only one
the men, taking turns, have not chosen.

Nearby, grain elevators lacking only
a spark of static electricity. The boy's
no sob sister, takes up the thick dowel
deeply stained. It's light in his hands.
In any world but this one
it would be like stepping up to the plate—
Stand in there, you're the man.

The end comes down on backbone
making his plaid cap with its dangling earflaps
fall over his eyes and his grip sting.
But he can take it. He digs in,
this time connecting on the sweet spot.

One leg broken by a trap, the thief's
unable to trot out much cunning, though
there's that henhouse gape to its jaws.
The last fox turns to face the boy,
and whatever passes between these two,
the snow on its way to furrows can't tell.

Hard Shakes and Homesteading

Look for New Madrid and you'll understand
why I'm living in a flatboat lapped
by winter weeds. The earthquake left it here
a mile from the river, unmanned, its bins
of potatoes tagged for New Orleans.
Good poplar and bur oak in the hull,
strong stanchions and tongue and groove overhead
when I sleep. A week ago this craft
was one among many in a floating town.
Ohio, Iowa, Kentucky, Illinois—all
lashed together in a cove above New Madrid
for fellowship and the bartering
of apples, whisky, tinware, hemp; for poker
on the sharpers' barge outlined with lanterns.
December 16, 1811 is the date on my deed
to a quarter-section of farmland west
of the settlement, and taking possession
at midnight of that very day,
swapping a mill town in Massachusetts
for the Main Chance, I began
chopping pine for a cabin. About 2:00 A.M.
I'd raised the axe to notch a ridgepole
when convulsions flowed up my body and the haft
so that even now in my hands I feel
the axe head rippling like a flag. In front of me
a field stone bobbing and jagging
like a panfish float, the land rolling
in troughs and crests, trees pitching like masts.
Then I was gone into the crevice, dark,
a slurry of foul odors, the air scalding.
It was the great comet come alive
and tunneling wildly through bedrock,
I now believe, the marvel that all November
gave a full moon's light until it plunged,
as Choctaw claim, into the Mississippi.

I awoke among clam shells,
the ground beneath me seamless again.
I ran choking from brimstone toward
the river and found it on the town common
pouring into fissures then geysering,
boiling and sucking. Islands in the channel
rose like mesas. At dawn New Madrid
was logs already well on their way
to New Orleans by the new river
route, but on my homestead this beautiful
potato barge rocking in the aftershocks.
I've gone like a seed into my own ground,
so what can I do but stay?
I know the signs. An hour ago I observed
panthers and deer crowded peaceably
into a clearing on my property, their
heads low, tongues lolling. I mean to ride out
the next set of shakes and all after.

Horror Flick

The shade afloat allows glare to pour
over the sill, then falls in backdraft
against the screen, tightening
sunlight through pinholes, so flak
buffets a balsawood Flying Fortress
hung on thread from the ceiling over
the bed where the boy lies doing nothing.
Through the ductwork and register come
his parents' voices from the living room
spiking and fading. Where can he go?
He doesn't want to listen anymore
to *layoff, mortgage, church envelopes.*
Once again his father lifts the storm door
and stomps down cellar steps. The world
outside takes a deep breath, darkening
the room as a workbench motor starts up,
and now an edge held to the emery wheel
howls into the furnace damper.
The boy's skin prickles as though
metal sparks rained down on him,
but it doesn't last long, that outcry.
What he fears is the silence now that
the blade is ready, the long wait
for the cellar door to open, his father
alive . . . He drifts back to that movie
the pastor showed last week to the seventh grade
in the school's new multipurpose
room. A horror flick: lit by lightning,
the family mausoleum stands ajar
—hoots and applause from the kids—
while inside the mansion where the master's
last will and testament is being read,
a secret panel moves. Then cut to
a young woman crossing this remoteness
alone when her car breaks down.

She's at the door now, pounding
the ring in the winged creature's mouth . . .
The phone line's dead, so she'll accept
refuge till morning . . . Nightgowned
in the room the butler chose for her,
she strokes the deep folds of drapery
pulled across casement windows
and turns to admire the chandelier.
Just then the camera zooms to
a man's bare feet and strips of winding sheet
glinting below the velvet curtain.
Arms find her waist but thunder buries
her writhing screams, her pleas.
Lying in bed in silence the boy
puts himself behind those drapes
each time for what happens next, before
the pastor looks up from his prayers.
Slowly she leans back, eyes fluttering
closed, mouth open but soundless,
rolling her hips and shoulders as the hands
advance. . . . The projector's beam
withdraws and lights come on (the cellar
door opens). The care of souls
makes the screen fly up on its roller.
A cinder block wall is the end of that.

The Overlook

Elkhard Our Trail Man, they call him
at the National Trust. Today he slashes
through strangler vines, positions stone
against erosion, and brings down
deadfall limbs to reach the overlook
where the master of a sugar estate
and his wife and children are buried
under raised marble slabs, the grounds
untended for two centuries.

Gathering flower seeds and rootstalk
for their garden, Elkhard and his wife
discovered the tombs. In this plot
of Antillean hummingbirds they
surprised each other and made love
on Willem Leverock, b. 1745 d. 1780,
did rubbings of his coat of arms
with their bare skin while plumes
of the censerbush blessed them.
That night she woke him, gasping
from her dream in which a chattel gave birth
alone on the master's vault,
her womb flowing over the legend.

Elkhard's done his reading.
The slaves who rose against Leverock
and fired his estate while the family slept
were run to this headland by hounds.
Each rebel killed himself in turn.
The last in the circle broke every weapon
but the one he turned on himself.
To reward those trackers,
planters castrated the dead
then pitched their bodies into the sea
and hallowed this place with marble.

He drives home a sign warning
not to touch the manchineel tree
—lean against it and the sap will raise
lash welts—then heads down the path,
stops only to pick some horsetail, a weed
body slaves employed to whisk
their masters and mistresses clean
after bowel movements. The bristles
will lie under glass with cane
cutlasses and talking drums in the new
museum between the duty-free mall
and the Emancipation Memorial.

Paper Wasp

The queen has unfurled her nest
like an umbrella hung by its tip
beneath the eaves. She wintered
alone in a nest somewhere, a grub
like the tongue of a bell,
and now where there was nothing
I look up into chambers, each
containing a single egg.
A founder of colonies,
she lives on honeydew from aphids.
She builds with willow bark
chewed to pulp, and this time
with another fiber as well.
Between the half-moon indented tabs
QR and S in the dictionary
on the screen porch where I was
writing a poem that had nothing
to do as yet with a paper
wasp, there's a ragged excavation,
a cavern the size of a thimble
where she lifted words into the light
for me, etymologies and all.

Day Trip: Climbing to Freedom's Gate

Working my way up by rootholds, I clear
a hairpin ledge and find a man leaning
against the stonework of a cistern,
his white hair aloft in the trade wind.
"Killy rilly," he says noting a bird's
alarm cry above us in the cloud forest,
then, "I'm Samuel Gordon." The sea
keeps on breaking its colors in a deep
cut between bluffs as he talks.

"That mention in *The Daily Antillean*
of this abandoned place—the fifty year
anniversary—bring you struggling up,
but no word there about our lives
or how we move down the mountain
to Windwardview." On his mother's side,
the Middle Passage; on his father's,
removal to a sugar estate in Jamaica
when Cromwell leveled Irish barns.
Families in Freedom's Gate went back
three hundred years to the founders,
runaways from indenture and chains
who brought Celtic ballads and canefield songs.
"When descendants made a house over,"
he says, "it stay on original stone."

He claps a hand on the cistern,
tells me how his legs and shoulders
used to be like lava rock from bearing
tubs of vegetables up the ladder road
from the harbor to wealthy households
in Windwardview. So when the council
voted away funds to maintain the path
to Freedom's Gate, he was ready.
Because the other men in that hamlet
shipped aboard inter-island freighters,

Samuel Gordon bore all eleven cottages
and foundations down the quarter mile.
"My payment? Barter and community."

I follow the few steps to where,
fifty years ago, he crossed a threshold.
Because memory is the marrow
that will carry a place, I
listen and watch like an apprentice
as he takes apart that dwelling
plank by plank, upright by upright,
down to the spiders and lost buttons,
down to the silences, odors, voices,
a woman singing as she cleans
a fish whose ivory, gilt, vermilion
lies bold on spread banana leaves,
down to the stones of the founders
and beyond. He straightens every nail.

His shoulders after moving the final stone
felt so light they seemed to lift him
and he couldn't sleep. So he used to go
in the middle of the night idling about
New Freedom's Gate, where he could hear
his carpentry settling back onto stone.
"And then," he says, "maybe a little rum
building in me, I stroll away
and sing among privilege folk to vex
the constable. 'You see a man,' I told him,
'will move you up the mountain free of charge.'"

Milk

Teacher has appointed him milkman,
so today there's no one but him
this many steps below ground, no one
in the coolness of the hallway's
cinder blocks glazed a pale green.
He stops a moment at the storeroom,
where windows near the ceiling
let in light upon boxes and sleeves,
years of chalk, erasers, paper,
and those white tablets for the urinals.
He hears long division overhead
and leaves the room. He keeps
jumping high as he can till at last
near the far end of the corridor
he grazes the hanging furnace duct.
In a room next to the stairwell
the cooler shudders, cycling on.
Fitting cartons into a wire basket
for each hand, he sees it all ahead,
as when a fourth-grader brought *him* milk:
kindergartners cross-legged on rugs
braided from rags and outgrown clothes;
and taped-up on windows, drawings
of trees and clouds and houses.
Above his head the principal's door
opens, the chair by the window pivots . . .
"And what do you have to say for yourself?"
Now the milkman is ready,
who has to be back for the next lesson.

Sea Wrack: West Indies

Timing my reach between waves,
each one rising from Friars Bay
like a parenthesis, I come up with
an arm's-length of driftwood
draped in kelp and step back.
A fragment of planking, salt-pallid,
treenails still in place.
Here among the sandpipers
working each comber for fish eggs,
their bills quick as
the sewing machines of sweat shops,
I turn that carpentry, that claimant
on imagination, over and over:
the Old World and the depths it went to.
Wave upon wave, the sun's
going down behind men in catboats
seining where a galleon
rode at anchor, whose flag
named this island. Missionaries
gone over the side of the longboat,
did they shriek like children
when these breakers tumbled
them and pulled over their eyes
the habits of their order?
They crawled ashore. They arose
from sea wrack, and the Word
filled them and emptied the forest.

Compensation

A man who plows pale stubble under
for the next crop, bearing down to drive
the share deep, draws children to follow him.
In buckets, in aprons, they gather
stones the soil brought forth in the year
since oxen broke the burlap and denim
grassland and whole families carried off
tangleroot limestone, flint, quartz
to make a mountain in Kansas.
The plowman turns his team. A boy holds up
a stone in both hands to show his mother,
who is coming toward him with the rest
of the women. Having threshed the first
harvest for bread, that leap of faith
from seed, they are pulling the plow.
Because their husbands mustered out
after Appomattox and took compensation
in prairie, eight yoke of women
grip wooden crossbars at their waists,
calico grazing the stubble. The oxen?
They're dragging timber for cabins.
As her mother goes by, a girl in the furrow
picks up a flat stone and lets others
tumble from her lap. She rubs the blackness
with her apron and suddenly it gives
back the village pond in Ohio she loved
skating on. Think of that,
finding such a treasure—you wouldn't
carry it to the mountain. The women turn
again, preparing the earth for their children.

Pan Blender Man

Pitch Lake is working its deep currents, fold
upon fold, stirring prehistoric trees and more
under the dough-springy surface. *Tread lightly.*
Keep moving. Last year a councilman wandered
from jackiron rum onto this gentleness and fell
asleep. He emerged a month later, soles of his shoes
first, to edify a Bible study tour group.

A man rolls a rusted oil drum to the lake's edge.
Scrapped at a nearby refinery, it'll sell
after blowtorch, calipers, hammer, emery wheel
do their work. King Pharaoh and Ibis
demand his creations for their calypso.
He's Blakely the pan master of Trinidad,
thin as pitch on a stick, and white-bearded.

He looks out over the waveless motion
vacant this Sunday afternoon so rum shops
can have their turn. As a young man he gouged out
the asphalt with a spade, loading carts
that hurried on soft tires to shore.
The rains topped off those cavities until
a baker's mix of clay, ash, oil seeped in again.
Blakely knows where his own grave is.

He misstepped into one of those pools, and pitch
took him by the ankles. The last of his breath gone
into unlacing his boots, he had a vision:
he was that Carib chief who killed a hummingbird
sacred to the gods—there's a stone carving of him
in a cloud forest ravine—then howled for mercy
as the lake rose over him and his villagers.

Blakely coughed out tarwater and gave notice,
though what hasn't quit is the fear
that any blacktop he crosses might prove

bottomless. At a calypso roadmarch
the next day he discovered his powers.
When competing bands had given way to
Ash Wednesday, he carried tones home in his head
and fashioned an array of steel drums.

This rusted salvage from Standard Oil?
He'll leave it at his workshop, then attend
to the Port of Spain panyards, a vacant lot
among dwellings built of driftwood
and tin signs for soft drinks, where musicians
rehearse for festival jump-ups. *Pan blender man,*
everyone calls out. The bass, cello, ping-
pong drums fall silent as he walks among them
tuning the universe with a ball peen hammer.

Wing Chair by the Window

"Widow's Pass, the Milwaukee Road,"
said the card my grandmother
presented at the ticket window.
I was nine that summer and half-fare.
"Joseph Miller, 40 Years,
Brotherhood of Railway Carpenters,"
said the tiepin I wore as
I walked the coach and parlor cars,
where tools my grandfather took down
from attic shelves and let me
hold, not long before a stroke
took from him their names and mine,
had brought out the grain of
hardwoods, light and dark.
Nothing was out of true
though he would have rubbed
scratches away with rottenstone.
I believed the wing chair
I fell asleep in kept the bright threads
of his apprenticeship. Hadn't
his long craft gone into routes for
the Chicago, Milwaukee, St. Paul & Pacific
Railroad Company and for me?
I loved being last awake with rain
against the double panes. Zigzag
measures unfolded and blades
cut across on their way
to the oilstone. Only once,
coming home near the end of summer
from the horsehair sofas of railroad widows,
did I awaken before light. Someone
was watching me from a mainliner
held like ours at a station
and bound where we had been. . . .

There was no other train. I had caught
myself reflected there, a traveler
I would never meet again.

Welcome to Leapers' Hill

With his sugarcane machete he leveled
a stand of thorns for the National Trust,
readying the suicide
view for High Season on Grenada.
From where Caribs leapt who would not
bow as prisoners for rising against
the French fort, a pod
seeding plantations in the trade winds,

this groundskeeper saw the year's usual
bedsprings, tires, shopping carts
among boulders that wear breaking waves
like the cowls of missionaries.
He knows a path to the sea
and brings the castoffs up to his truck,

then goes back to search tidal pools
for bones. These thirty years he's discovered
skulls and femurs and ribs—the leapers
who waited in cold bottom currents
three hundred years for a caretaker,
his Carib grandmother told him.

He carries them ledge by ledge up the escarpment
to a cave no one any longer
remembers. It holds a petroglyph
of a woman big with child, carved in outline
on a lava boulder like the ones
he maintains below. Standing
with arms upraised, round eyes and mouth
under a feathered headdress, she looked out
on sails blazoned with crosses,
on blunderbuss and armor.

No relics today, but he always visits
his gleanings and the goddess, celestial
and earthly womb, while

above them on the headland those coral
grottoes ringing the cemetery
have been vandalized, that once held
Madonna and child and the Apostles.
Watching a rain squall on the horizon

he remembers what his grandmother
taught him: when their bodies opened on stones
the souls of warriors leapt
into the sky and its gardens, where
they feed on cassava cakes. Pure
streams flow through the afterlife,
and the sea is a pool formed by waterfalls.

He rests his hand lightly on the navel
of cold stone beside him and feels
waves breaking, sunlit spume, the sea
bringing the bones of her own, her children,
for her child to find.

A Lake in the Pine Barrens

Because water keeps offering
transcendence, you can still
skip a stone across a lake
in the Pine Barrens. You can count
the stations along the line,
the beads in the chain. No matter
drought that turns lawns the color
of potato chips, the aquifer
keeps every lake in the Barrens
from falling. As you circle an acre
of water, its dark tea color the gift
of tannins leaching from cedar
roots, from needles and fleshy cones,
the soil underfoot could be passing
from the upper bulb of an hourglass.
While there are those who see
in every frond and fiddlehead
of cinnamon fern a regret
at not enhancing a property line,
you can still drink from your hands
this sweet obscurity that captains
of four-masted schooners knew
would hold its purity, its provenance,
from Cape May to the Canaries.
Looking at this water,
you can't be looking at anything else.

A Day at Zero

Snow squalling off the Mississippi,
the first place I could imagine
zero, stunned and wobbled me,
then sagged back onto the ice,
a remoteness where saints could have
wandered and been given signs.

I kept my footing on thick shallows
blown clear of snow, where the river
was like paraffin nubbly
with air bubbles, minor energies
on the sly, and where it made
such a level line against the bank
I could have signed my name.

Then a shrill cry turned me around.
A hawk rose from the bank with whiteness
twisting in talons: the weasel
I had just seen wrenching field mice
from their burrow, a family
given away by the thicket of hoarfrost
their breathing made at the entrance.

In the air they were one, a brown-winged
ermine pumping raggedly upriver
past floes caught at zero,
overriding one another to become
Nessie breaching. I drew even
as raptor and prey began circling
now more and more tightly above
channel ice and its marrow of current.
Their cries twined around them:
weasel disemboweling hawk,
whose bill hooked open the white throat.

They fell in the shape of a match head
spurting, and either I
or the ice trembled, or both.
A snow devil picked its way along,
gathering blood and plumage while I
kept my footing. I gave the day over
to a river that moved heaven and earth
to hold zero in place.

Game Day

Coal man who lowers a tin channel
like a playground slide through cellar windows
then hunches under a canvas basket,
he's come home, a stop on his route,
and what is he to make of his only son?
"What are you doing here?" the father
roars, leaning across the kitchen table,
thick fingers splayed. "What are you doing here?"
The boy doesn't know how to answer,
staring at those hands, but he's in fifth grade
and no one's going to make him cry.
At school he worked a case of fake chills
into a permission slip and came home
—his mother won't be back till supper—
to make lineups from baseball cards,
every player backed by his stats.
They're waiting in kitchen sunlight, stars
in sugary dust of the chewing gum
that comes with them. "Speak to me,"
the father says again, not moving his hands
from the table where at meal time
he speaks to no one. The boy's stomach
is quicksand as though he's watching from
the on-deck circle or kneeling again
in the confessional for the first time.
Last week his team visited the orphanage,
and after the game—he won it with a single—
while new friends were all having Kool-aid
in the dining hall, he closed his eyes and wished
he could live in the home for boys.
He won't say anything, staring at the table.
A twenty-game winner goes into his windup.
What can the father do now but turn
and fill the cellar bin, then go on with
his route, leaving handprints of coal?

Brethren of Salt

(Brigands' Cay, Bahamas)

On the ridge between tidewrack and abandoned
salina, the shapes you can spot
from open water—pirate lookouts?—
are a few spinebushes bulked up with
deposits from the trade winds skimming
the salt pan turned catarrhal by a rain squall.

In 1700, English deserters from indenture
settled this coral outcropping,
piped seawater over the ridge
with bilge pumps—what salt is here now
comes from storm surges flooding the pan—
then let the Tropic of Cancer
reduce the brine till they could rake it
into dunes Dutchmen needed in the holds
of herring fleets, so traded arms for.

"Where is the clause in Adam's will
saying the Caribbean is a Spanish lake?"
A galleon's captain would be greeted
with that challenge because beacons
atop the ridge had drawn him
from the sea-lane onto a sand bank.
The Brethren of Salt came aboard
tricked out in velvets and leather doublets,
with hemp fuses lit for the ship's
magazine and dangling from their beards.

They provisioned sailors in the longboats
but every officer got salted
with blunderbuss chambers of royal coin:
"In the sweet trade, no prey, no pay."
The loot found under stone ballast? Pearls,
conserves, ingots, silver church plate.
Till 1720, when a Spanish fleet
cannonaded the island and left grapeshot
mementos you can pry from coral.

On the ridge between breakers and salina,
where spinebushes stand like coast
watchers, the Brethren were tied to stakes,
eviscerated and stuffed with salt
and with handbills indicting them of
"innumerable insolences, lamentable incendiums."

Spring-Fed

Today among stalks of dieback
along the creek, these low
violet-and-white blossoms
like tiny hollyhocks mean
the pasque flower is here.
Earliest, it has the most names,
gifts from those who found it
in snowmelt: sleight of hand,
crown of mercy, hurryroot . . .
and nightbundling for the way
threads bind the petals.
What unfastenings at dawn,
the seed plumes being
themselves like moving water.
Newly free of ice, the creek
has deep pockets hoarding
roe and milt, keeping
dragonfly larvae for
when the shooting stars
are in flower along the banks
(stalks that in October
are rigged with spider webs
like sails—bound where?)
and a meadow lark
hops and bobs her head to
distract attention from her nest,
crying *see-you, see-you.*

Bitterness and Happiness

She is dancing the harvest
of cocoa beans dry in the sun,
her bare feet doing steps on a long
tray, one of a dozen women turning
and burnishing the seeds to mahogany
for Caribbean Produce, Inc.
The music she moves to is not here:
her husband playing the steel drums,
notes he could roughhouse or glissade
as she turned the harvest at
their own cocoa estate. "You
are the butterfly that followed us
as we gathered pods," he called out,
hurrying the sticks from pan to pan.
Hands on hips, she works her body
to be that blue morpho in the immortelles
planted to shade the cocoa trees,
immortelles whose flowerings are
the most lucid and passionate orange
in all the Antilles. He loved how in bed
her feet would exhale the day,
a bitterness to deepen happiness.
But he vanished in the hurricane
that took their small estate, leaving her
to shift work here, to slide, pivot,
balancing. Cocoa is *theobroma,*
"food of the gods," she told him
as they walked among cocoa blossoms,
those linen streamers
that prompted the weaving of lianas
into baskets for the bounty to come.
And in time the music
of steel pans, and she creating steps
now to follow him, now to lead.

A Man Inside a Tree in Nebraska

A man inside a tree in Nebraska is no
dryad, but a homesteader digging
his well through loam and clay and stone,
singing "Nearer My God to Thee."

As casing against cave-ins, the hollow
trunk of a black oak's desirable
for its girth and tight fibers
—to be lined afterward with stones—
and in a swale on his claim he found one.

With a mirror he angles dawn
into the well, marks the bottom
dry, so loads the bucket with tools
and lantern and cranks it down by windlass.
Before descending the ladder he gazes

out across his acreage, open prairie's
low swells and cross currents bounded
east and west by limestone ridges
like fastnesses the bluestem and dropseed

grasses break against. He's heard
about men overcome in wells
when they struck a pocket of noxious
vapors called the damps;

about settlers who buried their dead
—cholera, smallpox, typhus—in wells
because of scavenging wolves,
then abandoned their claims. Still,
what can he do but approach the water?

If not this well, then another.
Noon, and sunlight falling through the tree

makes the bedrock glow.
He finds himself in a furnace
bare-handing fire into a bucket

and thinking of his meal to come,
marrow from buffalo bones encased in
embers of buffalo chips. He'll be
a man in Nebraska with a well.

Weighing in Against Winter

Here's a creek payed out by springs
across a field, and the moon
catching hold. Late October, each
meander makes something to see,
lit to its bed of white stones
in the shallows. Ash
and beech going into the stream
trade the stories of their lives,
not a homily among them, not one
conspiracy theory. Bankside,
mushrooms like chimneys and macaroons,
a cinnamon fernscape, and here's
a contour of asters, rootstalks
weighing in against winter.
Between tall staghorns of sumac, stars
and the web of an orb-weaver
in ruins. If Perseus
slashed and brought down that web
in carrying the head of the Medusa away,
wasn't it time? Just here,
in moonlight, where the creek bed
gleams like a shovel
burnished through years of stoking,
the current pooling deeply
summons up a coalbin, and a man
awakening to unearth fire
from its bank of ashes. Nuggets
that will break the back of darkness
keep on rasping a kind of music as
they stream into the flames.
Years, you can have them for a song.